W9-CLB-274

This book belongs to:

My Travels with Clara

MARY TAVENER HOLMES

Illustrated by JON CANNELL

J. Paul Getty Museum
Los Angeles

Millis Public Library
Auburn Road
Millis, Mass. 02054

OCT 0 2 2007

It was love at first sight.

SHE WAS JUST A BABY, even though she was covered in iron plates and weighed a thousand pounds. She was looking right at me with her soft brown eyes, and she was not one bit afraid. *I wasn't afraid either.*

We had great adventures together.

THIS IS OUR TRUE STORY.

HER NAME WAS CLARA, and she was a rhinoceros. She was so young when she lost her parents. This was in India, in the late 1730s. A kind man took her into his house, where she walked carefully around the furniture and ate from plates.

Though tame as a kitten, she soon began to grow too big for her home. And so the man sold her to me, Douwe. *Douwe Van der Meer.*

I was a sea captain, from Holland, and I took Clara onto my boat, the good ship KNABENHOE. She was a fine sailor and lived on the Knabenhoe happily for six long months.

CLARA'S FIRST JOURNEY, *from* CALCUTTA *to* ROTTERDAM, 1741

Atlantic Ocean

FISH OIL

DIRECTIONS: APPLY AS NEEDED.

Really Stinks!

I WANTED CLARA to be comfortable and even made her a special skin lotion of fish oil and mud. She smelled *terrible*. She loved it.

HOLLAND
ROTTERDAM

EUROPE

INDIA

CALCUTTA

AFRICA

Indian Ocean

What, exactly, is a rhinoceros?

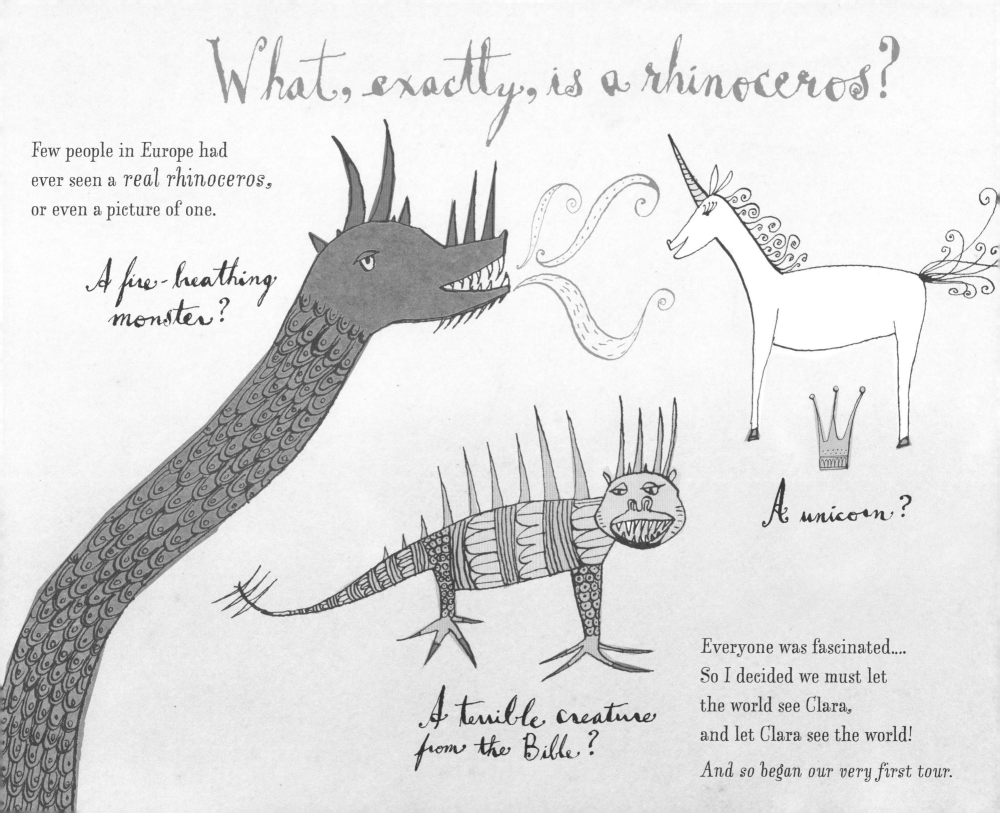

Few people in Europe had ever seen a *real rhinoceros*, or even a picture of one.

A fire-breathing monster?

A terrible creature from the Bible?

A unicorn?

Everyone was fascinated....
So I decided we must let the world see Clara, and let Clara see the world!

And so began our very first tour.

You must understand—a rhinoceros eats all the time. ALL THE TIME: *60 pounds of hay, 20 pounds of bread... washed down with 15 buckets of water... A DAY.*

Care and Feeding

60 LBS. of HAY

20 LBS. of BREAD

15 BUCKETS of WATER

There were certain things she loved.
ORANGES. She could never get
enough oranges.

And, strange as it seems, beer,
which I gave her from a bowl.
This made her burp.

She liked the smell of tobacco, and
if I had been smoking my pipe—or
eating an orange—she licked my face.
She had a soft tongue, like a puppy's.

The Amazing
CLARA
A LIVE RHINOCEROS!

I MADE A SPECIAL CRATE for her. The crate fit onto a wagon. The wagon had huge wheels, and a ramp for her to climb up and down. We needed eight strong horses to pull our wagon and its heavy passenger over the rough roads.

PLAN of OUR TRIP

ENGLAND

BERLIN

LEIPZIG

GERMANY

DRESDEN

• PARIS

VIENNA

FRANCE

AUSTRIA

SWITZERLAND

VENICE

ROME

ITALY

• = CITIES TO VISIT

Roade

River

BRIDGE

ALTERNATE ROUTE?

{ INVENTORY }

1. ORANGES
2. HAY = 60 lbs/day × ?? days
3. WATER
4. SOUVENIRS
   a. POSTERS
   b. MEDALS ← NEED TO DESIGN

Horses for Cart

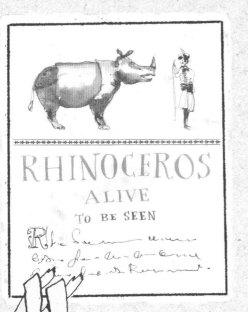

RHINOCEROS
ALIVE
TO BE SEEN

Me!

We pasted posters all over Europe, to let people know that Clara was coming to town, and when they could see her—from nine to noon and from two to six—and how much they would have to pay.

Finally, in the spring of 1746, we set out on our first tour—through Germany, Austria, and Switzerland.

Souvenirs

FREDERICK THE GREAT

Frederick was a great tipper, too!

12 ducats
+6 ducats
----
18 ducats

April: Berlin. Frederick the Great, the flute-playing ruler of Prussia, comes with his whole court to visit us and is astonished.

October: Vienna, the home of the powerful Habsburg family and of the Empress Maria Theresa.

She rushes to see Clara right away and is so amazed that she comes back with her children. The empress has her son's portrait painted with a book open to a picture of a rhinoceros.

EMPRESS
MARIA THERESA

MINIATURE
of ARCHDUKE KARL JOSEPH
SON of EMPRESS MARIA THERESA

Dresden: Augustus the Third, the Elector of Saxony, brings his son to see Clara. Like most people, Augustus falls in love with her.

AUGUSTUS the THIRD

AUGUSTUS HAD A FACTORY just for making porcelain—*beautiful, fragile porcelain.* Before you knew it, porcelain rhinoceroses began to appear all over Europe. I've also seen marble Claras, bronze Claras.... I've even seen her portrait on coins.

Made in the city of Meissen.

May 1747:

Leipzig. On the city's fairgrounds we weigh Clara by putting a big strap around her middle and lifting her up with cargo pulleys. She weighs almost five thousand pounds and is five feet seven inches tall and twelve feet long.

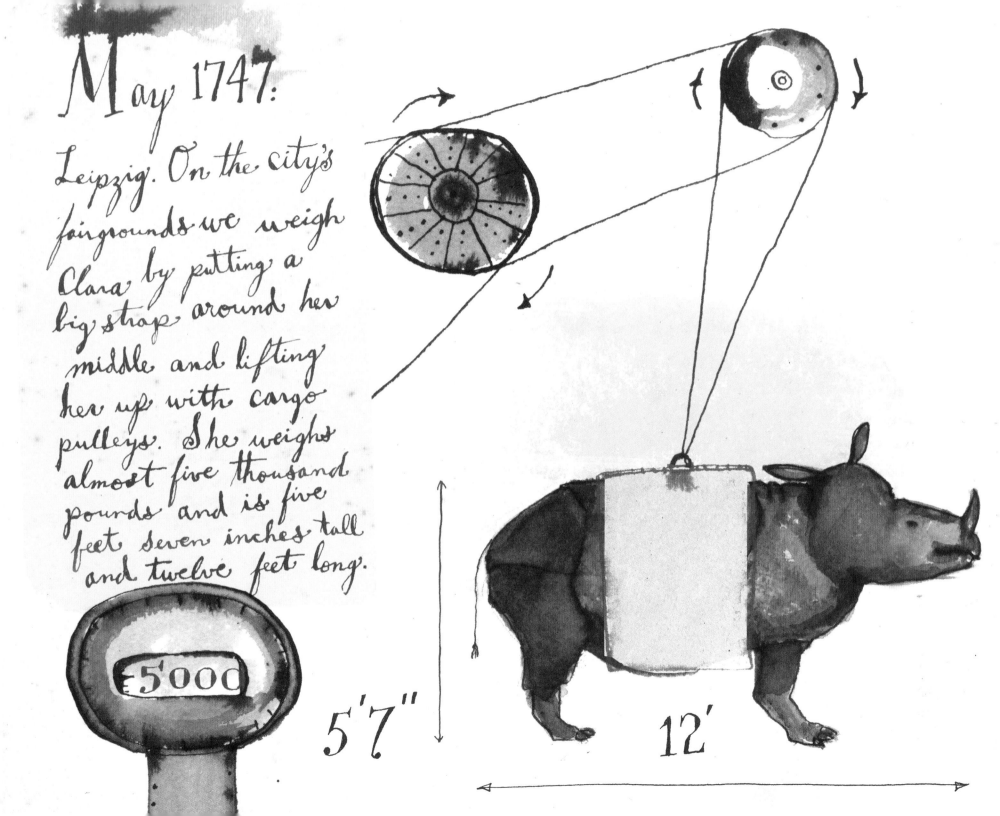

5000

5'7"

12'

BY THIS TIME Clara was becoming tired of traveling over bumpy roads. We spent our summer vacation in the place she loved the most of all: an orangery—a hothouse for raising oranges. Clara was in *rhino-heaven*, wandering among the sweet-smelling orange trees that produced her favorite food.

I HAD AN INSPIRATION:
Clara had been such a good sailor
on the Knabenhoe that I decided
to float her down the Rhine.

It was quite a sight, I must
admit: a rhinoceros floating
serenely on a timber raft on
that mighty river.

RHINO ON
THE RHINE

Along the Rhine

Versailles

1749 and a new destination: France.
We headed to Versailles, the great palace
outside of Paris, to visit King Louis XV.

LE SALON DE LA MENAGERIE que l'on voit icy par derriere est entouré d'une cour aussi de figure octogone, fermée de grilles de fer, qui la separe de sept autres cours remplies d'oiseaux rares, et d'autres animaux de divers païs eloignes. La prem.e cour à main gauche en entrant contient les escuries, les estables, et les bergeries dans la 3.e à main droitte est une voliere magnifique remplie de Pigeons de diverses especes curieuses. A Paris chez N. Langlois. Avec privilege du R.

The royal zoo in better days.

King Louis XV

No. 5 SEAL

No. 1 TIGER

No. 3 CAMEL

No. 2 LION

STILL NEED! No. 8 RHINOCEROS

No. 4 PELICAN

The dilapidated zoo at Versailles contained *one old camel*, *two wheezing lions, two tigers, a grumpy pelican, a seal....* Louis was very taken with Clara, and for a short time it looked like Clara might be moving in with the other animals! But I couldn't leave her there.

ON WE WENT to the glorious city of Paris. Never had I seen such a reaction. The whole city went crazy with...

Claramania!

I saw clocks that looked like Clara...

...hairstyles in the shape of rhino horns!

Rich people even dressed up their horses to look like Clara.

There were
beaded textiles.

Teapots and statues.

TEA

RHINOCEROS

RHINO

HORN
Nº 3

Writers and philosophers stared and
stared at her and then described her
in their big encyclopedias.

Fantastique!

Jean–Baptiste Oudry came to take a look at Clara. He had painted the king's hunting dogs; now he announced he was going to make a portrait of Clara, LIFE-SIZE. And so he did.

The soulful expression on her sweet rhinoceros face!

Rome

After our grand success in France, we decided to go to Italy.
By March of 1750, we were in Rome.

It was here that something terrible happened: CLARA LOST HER HORN. She must have rubbed it off on her crate.

For days and weeks I was afraid she was sick. And what were we going to do? A rhinoceros without a horn is not much of a rhinoceros.

I'm happy to report that her horn eventually grew back, just like human hair and fingernails do.

Oh no! Her horn came off!

From Rome we traveled north to Venice.

We arrived in time for the biggest party in all of Europe. It begins on the day after Christmas and continues for months and is called Carnival.

Venice

Gondola

Gondolier

Pietro Longhi was a friend of mine, and he painted this picture of Clara in her stall, being visited by people in their fantastic Carnival masks. (That's me on the right, puffing on my pipe.) The masks were made of papier-mâché. A half-mask was called a *bauta*. A full mask was called a *domino*, and you kept it on your face with a button that you held between your teeth.

Domino

My assistant holding the horn that fell off.

Bautas

Clara poop

Streets made of water

These are only a few of the things I remember from my travels with Clara, who lived to be about twenty years of age.

We were fellow sailors, traveling companions, and, really, friends. A day doesn't go by that I don't think about her.

I'm glad that the world had the opportunity to see Clara.

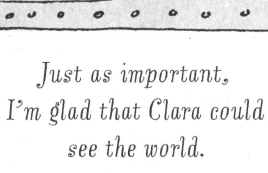

Just as important,
I'm glad that Clara could
see the world.

© 2007 J. Paul Getty Trust

Published by the J. Paul Getty Museum, Los Angeles
Getty Publications
1200 Getty Center Drive, Suite 500
Los Angeles, California 90049-1682
www.getty.edu

Mark Greenberg, *Editor in Chief*

John Harris, *Editor*
Jim Drobka, *Designer*
Elizabeth Zozom, *Production Coordinator*

LIBRARY OF CONGRESS
CATALOGING-IN-PUBLICATION DATA

Holmes, Mary Tavener.
  My travels with Clara / Mary Tavener Holmes ;
  illustrated by Jon Cannell.
    p. cm.
  ISBN 978-0-89236-880-8 (hardcover)
  1. Indian rhinoceros—Europe—Biography. I.
  Cannell, Jon. II. Title.
  QL737.U63H647 2007
  599.66'8'0929—dc22

                    2006035719

Printed in Singapore

Text paper is Senlis. It contains wood from well-managed
forests certified in accordance with the sustainable practices
of the PEFC (Programme for the Endorsement of Forest
Certification).

Mary Tavener Holmes is an independent scholar who lives in New York City. She is the author of numerous publications, including *Nicolas Lancret: Dance Before a Fountain* and *A Magic Mirror: The Portrait in France, 1700–1900*, with George T. M. Shackelford.

Jon Cannell is the owner of Jon Cannell Design and Illustration. He has worked for such clients as Starbucks Coffee Company, Chronicle Books, the *Harvard Business Review*, and UNICEF. He lives in North Bend, Washington.

Pronunciation Guide

Douwe Van der Meer ~ DOO-vuh van der mare

Knabenhoe ~ Kuh-NA-ben-hoo-eh

Leipzig ~ lipe-sig

Pietro Longhi ~ pe-EH-troh LON-ghee

Louis ~ lu-ee

Meissen ~ MY-sen

Jean-Baptiste Oudry ~ zhon bap-teest oo-dree

Versailles ~ ver-sigh

Illustrations

Jean-Daniel Kamm, *Medal for a Rhinoceros*, ca. 1748.
Silver, diam.: 1½ in. Historisches Museum Bern.

Possibly by or after Jean-Daniel Kamm,
Clara Commemorative Medal. Perhaps lead with a copper
core, diam.: 1⅝ in. Jeanne and Andrea Rothe.

Johann Joachim Kändler (German, 1706–1775),
Small Rhinoceros. Porcelain, 4⅛ x 7¹/₁₆ in.
Staatliche Kunstsammlungen Dresden, Porzellansammlung.

H. Oster, engraving after Anton August Beck (German,
1713–1787), *A True Delineation or Pourtraiture of a Living
Rhinoceros (by some called Unicorn)*, 1747. Ink on paper.
© Rijksprentenkabinet, Rijksmuseum, Amsterdam.

Maker unknown, *Beaded Panel*, ca. 1755 (detail).
Multicolored glass beads on a textile support,
12 ft. 8 ⁹/₁₆ in. x 1 ft. 7¹¹/₁₆ in. Bernard Steinitz, Paris.

Jean-Joseph de Saint-Germain (French, 1719–1791)
and François Viger (French, 1704–1784), *Rhinoceros
Musical Clock*, ca. 1750. Painted and gilt bronze,
enameled copper, glass, and wood veneered with
tortoiseshell; clock: 22⅞ x 15¾ x 7⅛ in. Paris,
Musée du Louvre, Département des Objets d'Art.
Gift of Monsieur and Madame René Grog-Carven,
1973. © Photo: Jean-Gilles Berizzi/Réunion des
Musées Nationaux/Art Resource, New York.

Nicolas Langlois (French, 1640–1703), *Vue générale de la
Ménagerie de Versailles*. Engraving. Versailles, Musée national
des châteaux de Versailles et du Trianon, inv. GRAV. 465.

Johann Joachim Kändler (German, 1706–1775),
A Turk Riding a Rhinoceros. Porcelain, polychrome enamel
decoration, gilding, 10⅜ x 10¹⁄₁₆ x 4½ in.
Historisches Museum Bern.

Jean–Baptiste Oudry (French, 1686–1755), *Rhinoceros*,
1749. Oil on canvas, 10 ft. ½ in. x 14 ft. 9⅛ in.
Staatliches Museum Schwerin.

Pietro Longhi (Italian, 1702–1785), *The Rhinoceros*,
ca. 1751. Oil on canvas, 24⁷⁄₁₆ x 19¹¹⁄₁₆ in.
Venice, Museo del Settecento Veneziano di
Ca' Rezzonico.

ADMIT ONE
Come See The Amazing
CLARA THE RHINOCEROS
TICKET No. 9
Presented by
DOUWE VAN DER MEER